# Nurture & Torture

**Lois Hirshkowitz**

POEMS IN THESE PAGES HAVE APPEARED IN
*American Writing:* "Tivoli."
*Journal of New Jersey Poets:* "Nurturer-Torturer."
*The Laurel Review:* "Afternoon."
*The Louisiana Review:* "Not an Elegy, Yet."
*O.C. Observer:* "To My Son Who is Getting Married in Two Days."
*Poetry Australia:* "Euthanasia," "Wings of Desire."
*Without Halos:* "Euthanasia," "The Question."


Special thanks to Sandy Hirshkowitz for use of the sculpture "Persistence" in the cover photograph.

Cover design by Lisa Anselmo.

Cover photograph by Jan Frank.

    Copyright: Lois Hirshkowitz, 1992
    ISBN: 0-931289-09-2
    Library of Congress Catalog No: 91-66343


SAN DIEGO POETS PRESS
P.O. Box 8638
La Jolla, California 92038
Kathleen Iddings, Editor/Publisher

To My Mother

# Table of Contents

Nurturer—Torturer / 9

### I. ONE MORE JOKE

One More Joke / 13
*After Fay's Third Operation* / 14
*Happy New Year* / 14
*The Hospital Vigil* / 15
*Last Rite* / 15
*The Waste of It* / 16
*Who is Sylvia* / 16
*Joey* / 17
The Unveiling / 18

### II. WINGS AND DESIRES

On the Ninth Day / 21
Other Ways To Get Home / 22
Wings of Desire / 23
A Head's Aches / 24
Cystoscopy / 25
Afternoon / 26
Mad Dogs / 27

Two for Fifty-Five / 28
In Medias Res / 29
After Auschwitz / 31
Pin the Tail / 32

III. TELLING TIME

Telling Time / 35
Passerine / 36
Dead Ends / 37
Spirit Song / 38
Gigantomastia / 39
Camino Real / 40
To My Son Who is Getting Married in Two Days / 43
Libation / 44
Euthanasia / 46

IV. NOT AN ELEGY

84 / 49
*Two Pounds of Flesh* / 49
*The Anniversary* / 49
*The Album* / 50

*Mothers* / 50
*The Graduation* / 51
*Brothers and Sisters* / 51
*The Birthday* / 52
*The Funeral* / 52
Eight, at Least / 53
Their Quality of Life / 55
Nails / 57
Tivoli / 58
Passover / 59
I'm Dying, You're Not / 61
What's Left of the Moon and My Mother / 62
Not an Elegy, Yet / 63
*Dies supremus* / 64

### V. QUESTIONS

The Question / 67
Is this the Poem? / 68
Who Knows? / 70
Way To Go / 73
Multiples / 74

# Nurturer—Torturer

1.

In Room 422 there's hardly enough light
to see my old friend, Fay. Better that way,
her hair off, dentures out, her lips cracked,
the tubes that rise and fall, her breath inside
them. I wet a gauze sponge, drip it across
her mouth. She stirs, starts to open her eyes,
tries to say something. Her tongue is paper.
Try a sip of water, I beg, it will make
you feel better. She lifts her hand, shakes
a no, no thank you. Her eyes close, her breathing
so shallow and when she starts heaving
up air in gasps, I lift her, gently lift
her, gently lift the straw, push it in,
soundlessly she pulls. Again, Fay, again.


2.

Watch his teeth, he's snapping, watch your fingers.
If we look away, he'll shrink, can't weigh more
than a pound or two, he's as kitten small
as he was first time sitting on your head.
He's sniffing it. Grab his jaw. Pry his mouth
open. Pop the pain killer in, that
tablet. Now the cream to wash it down.
You hold him. I'll release the dropper. There
one drip, two. Shred the chicken. Look he's licking
it. Let's try to drop it in. Hold him,
don't let go. Don't hear his shrieks, his howls.
Don't see his wide eyes. Don't let him go.
Don't even think, will it ever be fun
for him to be Leo cat again?

3.

Why do you say that, Mother, I'm not forcing
you to eat. I'm uncovering the dishes
and looking in. Maybe something's tempting
in here or in that one, something delicious-
looking. Yes, you're right, everything needs salt,
coronary patients can't have salt. Taste
some broth, spoon up carrots and peas, catch
a noodle, a potato. Look, roasted
chicken breast, golden and shiny. Easy,
you've stuffed your mouth. Forgotten how to eat?
Cut it, chew it, swallow. There, a small piece,
now a sip of tea, you and I are not geese.
Don't gag. You've had enough? I'll take the cherry
pie, chicken, the rice, your soup. I'll sip your tea.


4.

Eat for Mommy, just a little, a tiny
bite, a corner of the cracker. Open,
a sip, one drip. You can't go so
long without eating — we won't be back home
for another two weeks. The food in
Canada is the same as ours, American
cheese, Canadian cheese, what's the difference,
my baby, it's just a cracker. Milk is milk.
Take it, that's it. Tiny bits, no gagging.
Again, try it again. Tired? Rest your head
on my lap. I know you like the taste at home.
Want a story, love? Remember the time
you ate at Auntie Bev's house, didn't she cook
a seafood ragout for you. Didn't you look?

# I. ONE MORE JOKE

# One More Joke

I know what's in store for me
as I'll sit with Fay
and hold her hand.
She will let me sit,
but she won't let me weep
watching her die of cancer.

Her speech is so slow,
and she will have to tell me
one more long story,
and I shall have to wait out
her pauses and laugh at last.

"Coming tomorrow?" She will say,
"When you come, I'll tell you
where I hid the money."
And she will always have
one more joke, won't she?
She will have to.

## 1. *After Fay's Third Operation*

Who is that toothless old thing, pillow-
propped, tied to this mechanical bed? Whose
gray fuzz, whose pink scalp. Fay, is that you?
What did you say? Yes, alive, no, not at home.
Don't turn. Your wig is here on the stand—
I brushed it for you this morning. Lips parched?
Let me wet your mouth. No, you cannot drink
yet. Easy, don't jolt the dark blood oozing
in and out of the tubes. Stick out your tongue,
I'll wet it with this cotton. Remember
the chocolate ice cream I brown-bagged and
sneaked in last night? Let's play our silly game.
Lift the flaps. Dip in the spoon. Open
wide. Feel it, cool and sweet. Want to, again?

## 2. *Happy New Year*

Today, Fay, you must eat sweets—it's Rosh
Hashanah. Today, in shul, we were counted,
who shall live and who shall die. No, the lox
isn't salty. Taste it. Eat whatever
you want—herring, white fish, challah, butter.
Today nothing can hurt us, we faced east,
chanted the Amidah, bent our knees,
looked away as the Kohaneem blessed us.
Taste the taglach, dip your apple slice
in the honey, drink the wine. Of course,
you'll live to go to Florida this
winter, why not. You're not dead in two weeks
and two days. Look at me. I won't let you.
Stop that. Stand up straight. Fay, fight, damn you.

## 3. The Hospital Vigil

Two or three days before Fay stopped talking
altogether, she had to use her
body to suck in a strawful of air.
Each time she wanted to start speaking
she opened her eyes and pulled me close
to her. "I was some bookkeeper," she gasped,
"everything perfect, never made a mistake."
I stroked her hand, "Of course, you were, what else?"
That was Tuesday. On Wednesday I ran late,
still in my day when I got there. She knew,
"You look tired," Fay took my hand, pressed it
and whispered, "I'll never forget you
as long as I live, and you know I don't lie."
This then the moment Fay began to die.

## 4. Last Rite

The two car procession pulled out at ten.
You and Zig rode in the Lincoln, you in
your white shroud and veil, Zig in his raincoat.
I was behind, playing Handel for you.
At eleven, the clouds are puffs, and we move
into the right lane. At exit sixteen
the geese do a virginia reel,
and a dead squirrel is pasted to the road.
I put on my dark glasses, I tell you, Fay,
close your eyes, the sun is all over us.
That's when I remembered, you never ate
that lobster. You never cracked its claws,
never pulled the slippery meat of it out,
and I said, shit, Fay, "I'm sorry," aloud.

15

## 5. *The Waste of It*

The waste of it. Zig paid six hundred
dollars to a rabbi he doesn't know
and you didn't know, a total stranger
to say Kaddish every day for you.
Didn't he know I'd do it for nothing?
How could I forget you? Others, too. Jan
and Holly Kokes were at our house last month.
We miss Fay, they said. Yes, they know you're gone.
What a lady, what a shame she's gone.
And after Thanksgiving dinner, when
our kids took the other old ones home,
when Archie and I cleared the table,
we passed and touched arms, we reflected and sighed,
we looked up. "Fay," I said and "Fay," he replied.

## 6. *Who is Sylvia?*

We were eating dessert, when a cold wind
touched me. I turned. No, no one had walked in,
no door had closed, just the letter from Ziggy.
Your Zig, bowtie and all, tanned. How silly
to have worried. Sylvia is minding
him. Sister Sylvia, your brother's widow,
in Florida. Did you know that she drives
her Ford Tempo like a man, that she is kind,
has a wonderful disposition? And look
at this, she is an excellent cook.
Who could ask for anything more — a no strings-
attached arrangement. Zig can stay as long
as he wants. Will he try chocolate ice cream
next? Have you seen your brother? Go ahead. Scream.

# 7. Joey

Move over, Fay. Here comes Joey. AIDS this time.
Dearest Fay, I borrowed you for this while;
now I give you to him. No, you never
met him: sunlight brown eyes and curls, that smile,
too young to be the child you never had
here. Fay, take Joey in your arms. Rock him.
Tell him a story. Let him tell you one.
I can hear the two of you at it,
one, two, you'll see. His rabbi, the service,
so dull, no mention of AIDS. But that's between us,
Fay. You make Joey laugh, tell him this:
as the rabbi read the prayer, a nasty rip
started running down and then up my thigh
and then into my groin as I rose to say goodbye.

# The Unveiling

This morning I had pulled stems
and leaves from a pint of Jersey
blueberries, picked out the soft
ones, already white at the center,
saved the best, the firmest,
washed them and shined them,
ate some for breakfast.

It's late afternoon now and we're
on the way home after lifting
the gauze from the headstone.
My white haired little mother
sits in the back of my car
and sighs and sighs, "I'm so happy."
She answers, "I'm happy you're
not leaving me there, not yet."

There, after the rabbi chanted the prayer,
my mother bent down and placed
a stone on our friend Fay's grave.
She whispered, "May the weight
of this keep your spirit still."
The customary stone, the customary
prayer, rest. Some others said it.

When it was my turn I reached into
my coat pocket for the plastic bag
filled with the best in the pint,
looked at a few, picked one, left it,
one shiny berry that rolled right off
and followed me home.

# II. WINGS and DESIRES

# On the Ninth Day

Adam sees Eve, far away.
She tosses her auburn hair
from one shoulder to the other,
leaps into her shadow.
"Hello, Adam," she whispers as she runs by.
"Eve," Adam calls, "look what I have.

"I have saved this for you.
Eve, sit here with me. See, our tree
will fan us and how soft this down is.
Touch it."
Eve strokes the snake.
She takes it in her hands.

"Eve, look it is dark,
where is our sun?"
Eve takes Adam's hand to the place
where the snake entered her,
"Here." And a red globe grows
fruit and skin within her,
the tree sheds its leaves.

Eve lies down, the pink-edged sky
her pillow, the leaves her sheet.
She calls, "Adam, look what I have
for you." She spreads her legs and
pushes down. Adam sees the red ball
sliding toward him.
He eats it, at last.

# Other Ways to Get Home

Until I was thirteen I was so straight a stick I
couldn't keep a skirt at my waist without suspenders.
There, I sat at noon, every week day, with Helen Trent
and Our Gal Sunday. Eat, my mother would plead, and I
would listen to her and Helen Trent and Our Gal Sun-
day, and as I sat and chewed, I found and spat, left a
garland around the plate: lumps, bones, fat, gristle, and seeds.
What else could I do with Monday's ketchup covered
spaghetti, the Tuesday lamb chop, Wednesday's mound of
unseasoned ground beef, Thursday's slice of liver flavored
leather, and every day those potatoes mashed until
they were lumpy, and always something greenish on my plate.

I could dream about sky blue in a bottle and the man
with rough, cold fingers who sprinkled the blue into the
disappearing scraped ice. The germs, she feared, the color.
At five minutes to one, I left, walked across the street
to school, walked slowly, still working at finishing my
lunch, eating my dessert banana sideways, sometimes
pretending each nibble a sweet explosion of corn
juice, sometimes the salty brine of the half-sour pickle
I tasted finally at fourteen, walking the mile on
Flatbush Avenue from my new school, my bus fare saved
school day after school day for my forbidden fruits.

One afternoon I saw her walking toward me, my mother
taking a walk this spring afternoon, a window
shopping spree. What else to do? I dropped my green pickle
into the gutter, did she see it? smell it? The garlic
of it. We never said, just walked the way home, somewhat
shriven, somewhat not. She talked freshly strained applesauce
cooling on the sink, Aunt Sophie's strudel, a glass of
milk. I was thinking pizza on Bedford? Knishes on
Rogers? Nostrand Avenue? Egg rolls on Tuesdays, five
fares. Chow mein on Fridays, ten fares. She was talking, what
would you like with supper tonight. She was not asking.

# Wings of Desire

Was it the movie that did it? To tell
the truth, I don't remember much of it:
a man wearing an overcoat with wings, perched
on a roof; a trapeze artist swinging
up and back for the last time, the circus
is closing. I touch the air, all around me
in waves, the nausea, my head aching.
I'm so sleepy, I must leave. Behind us
a wide aisle. I'm up, then down on my knees,
up again. I rush out the double doors,
and I am lying in my own wet,
shooting my own movie. Can you see me?
Squeeze my finger, my husband's fingers
on my neck. Say something, my daughter pleads.
Not yet, I can't. I must watch her at fifteen
coming out of anaesthesia, crying
and thrashing. I'm going to faint, I had thought.
Switch the scene. I'm fifteen and I'm changing
the dressing on a patch of poison sumac
blisters, oozing blisters, and when I lift
the gauze, the itch that rages through and through
my hand and I feel faint. I'm alright, I say,
I'm so hot. My husband unbuttons my shirt.
That's not what I mean. I'm aroused. I'm erect
inside my wet, I mean. He's careful
when he lifts me, walks me out, calls a cab,
my hair over my face, into his, my daughter
holding me up, my jacket half off,
my pants there and wet and heavy. At last
in the taxi. I cross my legs, squeeze down, pinch me
inside me, close my eyes, the five minute
ride on the cold leather seat, the more I press
the more I throb. At home his fingers on
my pulse again. Your color's gone, he says.
I say, I know where it went. We peel my clothes
off me, stand me in the shower. He waits
inside the room. I'm warm. I say I must go
to bed. He says, sleep baby, sleep, strokes
my hair, asks me how's my head, I banged it
when I fell. He tells me the story, read it
somewhere. In the end, the angel, the one
on the roof, gives up his wings, becomes a man.

# A Head's Aches

How quiet the light at six. (What is this?)
Who can peel a pink veil off the sun at six.
If only this ache would lift. I'm forehead thick,
my head (Caught?) in this sixth-hour contraction,
(My head?) an unmitigated weight.
I must, (Know) no not yet, I must lift it,
push it out, (whatever) there, (it is.)
inside: whatever confrontation, what-
ever I-am-wrong-you-are-right; or is it,
I-am-not-you-are; or is it let-us-
~~capitulate~~ (Silly me,) recapitulate.
I'm wound in this sheet. (I can outwit it.)
I'll sit up slowly, heads up, I'll make it
slowly, I'll do it, I'll do it. (Do it.)

# Cystoscopy

He squeezes a two foot tube into your urethra,
expands your purse until you are full up
to pain. Would that he let you out of stirrups,
let you press your thighs into—he's forcing
it into your deep, says he has it high
into the right ureter he knows is blocked
but he doesn't know why. The words he finds:
breathe, don't breathe as he snakes up
to the exact spot—expedient snake—
for the best picture. Shutter-open you snap
your own, aren't they called dogtooth that start
to bloom there at the snow's edge. It's March
on that mountainside. All summer they will bloom there,
and aren't you still breathing, and you are still here.

# Afternoon

When you are at eleven you want
to go skipping down a Sunday morning
holding hands, you and your dad,
filling all arms with heavy newspapers,
with fresh bread and cakes
that tease the two of you
to rush home and play.
One Sunday afternoon
seconds before the skipping must stop,
you and your cousin sit
playing cards on a sofa
three feet away from
your parents who sit
sipping tea and chatting.
It's lovely when your cousin takes
a card and leaves the hand
in your lap there
where it is warm, waiting.
Minutes later, it is half past eleven,
and your best friend and you are
almost asleep in her bed;
an inadvertent brush
of her hands on your almost
flat breasts leads you
to play with hers,
already developed and
firm and beautiful.
Walking alone from the newsstand
that Sunday, the next morning,
you remember the baths
he gave you, his little girl,
and the last bath only minutes ago.
Was it only minutes ago?
It feels cold in the dim evenings
when your dad leaves you alone in the bungalow,
when he joins his friends,
when it is now night, after night,
and Danny's grandpa enters.
His raspy voice breathes out puffs
of old cigarettes, his old rough
hands run up and down your body.
He thinks you are asleep
so you don't cry out. You wait.
And you will wait in the dark,
for hours.

# Mad Dogs

Now I watch where I walk, never know when
a Doberman will jump out of sound sleep
in the shade to grab my thigh. If only
he would bark first, then I could jump to get
away or run away, but he doesn't
and I do not, and he gets me and won't
leave me. My left leg throbs, so I limp and
I scream, he bit me, god damn it.
The workmen on the hill wake up, stand, look
at me, their hands shading their eyes. I look
at them, the dog's teeth are still bared, my blood
on his canines, please let his rope hold.
How will I get out of here, I can't run,
I stand there bleeding in the noon day sun.

# Two for Fifty-Five

Boobs and tubes, they call us. Tits and wieners.
I cook the hot dogs, he snaps your mammo-
gram. Sure he's a doctor, here's his diploma.
Look how cheap we are, one tit for thirty,
two for fifty-five. The hot dog is free.
We're a small operation, just the two of us,
reader and feeder. Will you want relish?
How he can read tits is a mystery
to me, how he can find a hot spot, buried
in the dark side of the moon to me.
Why wait? Do it today. Tomorrow we pack
up, move our truck again. Can't stay here, folks
here know he calls the shots, he knows who will croak.
They know I feed the present, I do the books.

# In Media Res

It's only Thursday but we're returning home:
damned Planning Board. I ache to be ushered into
a red velvet seat, served a chilled white bordeaux
and I'd spread soft butter onto crisp brown bread,
bite into it, sip it, yes it's cool enough,
yes, we listen in the car, what is new. Four
new classrooms and two bathrooms for sixty young
bodies, small bodies, plenty of room, add them
onto an existing building, shouldn't take
too long, but I worry, how is the sick cat?
Where did feline leukemia come from?
Yes, she is still sick, walks on trembling feet,
a skeleton with a fur wrap. Another
sweet little cat dying. I'm running late
for my yearly internal, thinking cat and
classrooms, and when he says, what have we here, my
pelvis tumescent? something? an ovary?
my uterus retrograde? Tomorrow a test,
we'll see. We're hopeful, the cat drank water
from the faucet. We put her downstairs. We go

at eight, the Planning Board memo said, eight sharp,
our site plan second on the agenda. Should have
come at five to ten, Briarcrest East is first.
Not our problem how much water they will use,
didn't they submit a recharge analysis?
(The environmental vice-chair walks over,
doesn't like the wording of our engineer's
request for a waiver.) Who cares Briarcrest must
plant five and a half inch trees, not yews, they're not
hardy enough, maybe Chinese junipers,
(our attorney and engineer didn't know
there would be a complaint from this environ-
mental chair, Smitty, they called him, Mr. Smith) not
high but wide, five and a half inches trunk wide,
grown trees, expensive. (The driveway on our site
plan looks narrow, hasn't the engineer made
the change?) Change your plans, Briarcrest East, resubmit
next month, it is ten o'clock, it is our turn,
everyone is tired and ready to go
home. That's why we got their approval so quickly,
that and the promises we made that the
secretary recorded on her machine that clicked

and clicked at us all this Thursday evening.

We are home by eleven. I open the clasp
of my watch, it was my grandmother's, gently
set it on the dresser, and when my cat howls
and I jump, I knock it off. So the cat *is*
still alive. The works go one way, the glass the
other. He goes down to check, she had howled, and
when he comes up to tell me that he needs a
plastic bag, she had died, I have already
put the watch together. I'm in the middle
of counting my papers when he says, she's dead,
sixty-two, sixty-three, that's it? Finis?

# After Auschwitz

On Elena's rosewood bureau
lie ten mauve gloves,
ready.

Her guests should not touch
these hands. This pair
will serve hot broth.

She slips her fingers
into the soft separations
and when she thinks she see

the blood seep into the gloves,
she passes serenely
past her panelled dining room

overlooking the park.
In the steamy air of her stove
she feels the warmth throb

through silk to tingling quick
to the broth as it moves
from one side of the server to the other.

Her hands perfectly tipped,
tipped red to perfection,
carry the silver tureen.

The double doors open wide,
she stands silent.
Her patient guests look up to her,

she smiles down.
The dark broth is bubbling.
It is time, dinner is served.

# Pin the Tail

Near the sherry, a list for me, chopped meat
and milk. Monday's unopened mail. Was it
Monday, Andy felt a lump, said it hurts,
when our doctor whispered it? What is cancer?
Andy asked and off they went. What time is it?
Ten? His leg is going now, off, drops
to the floor in a plastic bag, his leg
zippered into the plastic bag, tossed
onto the truck, mixed with chicken gristle,
broken sticks and stones. A sip to his health
and four and twenty tumors sitting in
the lab. Does my boy's thigh throb and jump?
What's a mother to do? To your health, children.
Turn and turn. Close your eyes. Don't look under.

# III. TELLING TIME

# Telling Time

We were stopped at a light
when he asked, "Would you be
twenty-five, incomplete again?"
I smiled back, "My love,
I am still filling at fifty."
It was eight o'clock and we faced
an evening sky, still pink at the edge,
an April evening, suddenly warm.

That's when he gave me
the gold watch. I held it, an old one,
set it, wound it gently,
one turn around. I slipped
the long gold chain over my head.
Whose gold watch on my chest now?
Was it his grandmother's?

There, she is sitting at her dressing table,
he behind her, waiting for the moment,
lifting her hair. There, the gold chain,
and on her lace bodice, the watch.
"Oh, my dear," she must have said,
"the etching on the case is lovely —
the trees, the lake, the cottage,
oh, it is our cottage."

"Lake George?" I asked. In our log cabin,
twenty-five years ago, the two of us,
alone at the lake, walking under trees
sprayed red and orange. We needed to be
alone, the tiny spots of blood
I left in the toilet. The two of us
waiting it out, wanting it — our son.
Yes, it is, yes, Lake George.

A few seconds later we reached
the restaurant on Hope Road
and the dark came down on us,
lifting the warmth with it.
And didn't I say, so it is,
it's eight o'clock again,
another evening, after all.

# Passerine

When I turn away you will disappear.
Should I ask you to stay?
I miss you only when you are here.

Why go now? At this moment of my year
that stores, no, steals returning days?
When I turn away you disappear.

We tease for smiles, we stand too near,
your black strands clinging to my gray.
I miss you when you are here.

One night next month will a restaurant mirror
play a trick? No, I'll say, but I'll gaze;
I turn away. You will disappear.

In the airport we confuse our fears,
we pass the salt to pass the hour's play.
I miss you, and you are here.

Too far, can't phone, we'll write to share
this year. I shall not ask, son, stay.
When I turn away you will disappear.
I miss you only when you are here.

# Dead Ends

Chaim stops slicing the lox to say to us
now he knows how I looked at her age
and when we walk out of the crowded store
we hear whispers of mother-daughter-
mother-daughter. Are they watching
the long flat backs of us and half the way
the long wavy hairs pulled up and back,
hers a fuller bush, a rich, dark roast,
mine more like weak tea. This morning
I pulled two or three tangled hairs out
of the brush she brought for me, told me
to try it on the wet knots too, told me
I wouldn't pull so many hairs out.
What is she doing? What's wrong now?
I listen to her damn it, her fuck, her look
at this, her bursting into my room,
look at this. She shows me four or five straight
hairs that grew in while she slept, I see four
or five black dots on her chin, I point
to my tweezers, and why, she asks, should she
have to shave hairs at the root of her toes
and why the fuzz on the inside of her thighs.
I stand at the long mirror, tugging at
matted hair, is the brush helping, she asks.
I know why. Why it helps? No, why you have hair.
Thanks a lot. You're welcome. She is at my
bathroom mirror, at my tweezers, and should she
change her job, try tax law, and should she
move, and I'm worrying about my letter
of resignation, when to give it to them
and should I tell my faculty first, I'm tired
and her apartment is so noisy, should she
move and do you or don't you want a camera
for your birthday, and should we or shouldn't
we snip off dead ends today or tomorrow,
let's just think about it today, and
it's so reassuring to know it isn't
any better to be her age, except
for that flat belly, it's all the same.

# Spirit Song

My son shows me his newest acquisitions
for climbing: snarg, hexentric, camelot.
He tells me to look up, look, the sun
is on Rainier. All I see are spreading clouds.
He used the snarg, he tells me, screwed the blunt
end into the ice, put the rope into it,
pulled his partner up. He's steady, they don't
fall into the crevasse. Sixty-five feet.
Twenty six and he must tell me this story.
When he was three and I left him for a week,
he turned into a dragon for the week,
crept along his bedroom floor and mine, pulls
himself along rockface now and waterfall
into clouds where butterflies brush his hair.

# Gigantomastia

Some people like big tits. My sister beamed when
her husband announced that hers were getting rounder
and fuller from all the massaging he did.
She was impressed that my daughter had them
at fourteen, where did she get them? I was startled
that one morning the child wakes up and there
they are. Not from me. They weren't from me,
two D-cup tits, didn't bind mine down, squeeze
them into a C-cup bra. From her aunt, that's where.
Do I hide mine under black shirts and jackets two sizes
too big, that and the ace bandage she bought for
working out and running, that, and then this mammoplasty.
The night before, my daughter's friends crowd around her,
bring her balloons, she laughs, they leave. I'll go soon.
She lifts two pink balloons from the bag, plays.
Think of what you will lose, I plead,
how will you know touch from touch. Think
what I will lose, she pleads. And you might have
scars.I have scars now, tears here and here.
She lifts her shirt, loosens her bra, shows me.
Now? she asks, passes a straight pin to me.
One, two, the pieces of pink plastic fall into
our open hands. So that's that. I hold her
in my arms, wipe a dot from her chin, remember
when it was I wiped a drop of my milk from her,
she so warm, her sweet breath tickling the fuzz
on my arms, she minutes out, or seconds, out of me.

# Camino Real

1.

Early in the morning on our terrace
before the sun creeps in, I sip my first
cup of hot coffee, plan my afternoon,
where shall I go today? I am warm,
I unbutton my robe. When will our linens
be changed? Are they already? I glance down,
one breast is out. I start to throb waiting
for him. To Zihuatanejo for dinner?
It will be too hot to go, no, too far,
we'll swim here in our own Pacific waters,
and I'll be the thin-waisted, C-cup, richly
tanned lady wearing a string bikini
who runs up the flight of stone steps from the beach.
Everyone will stare and touch me as I leave.


2.

It's the quiet of it I like, sitting
with him here at dusk, touching his hand.
An hour ago five groups of others
cluttered up the beach. Finally, gone.
Now we can listen for the crescendo
of high tide and read. As I turn the page
I look up to see how close we are.
There, look there, the same young couple, showing
us, he touching her hair, she running
sand through and through her fingers, turning
to him, her red strapless top turning.
Is this the moment to ask. Dine with us?
After, you and we shall love the dark cool,
each in the sheets of our shuttered room.

3.

I am sleepy. The spray from the water
cools and cools the sweat on my neck and breasts.
I close my eyes, let the breezes cover
my lids. I hold still, wait for the next
one and the next to press out the wrinkles
of my untidy cloth, up and tighter,
and younger and smoother. The sand and sun
are flickering lightly now. I let them
drop, the book and his hand, wait for one more.
"What can these tracks be?" I hear her, that lithe
young thing in red, singing out to me. "Up high,
here in the rocks." She is holding her straw
hat with one hand, pointing with the other.
She bends down on her knees, "Here, come closer."


4.

Her bright blue eyes look at me. Thirty-five
or more? Close up, deep lines around her eyes
and mouth. She laughs, "I was looking for
beautiful rocks for my little girl." My
little girl is twenty-three, I laugh. "Look."
Tiny points in the sand two by two,
rows and curving aisles stretch ahead
into enormous leaves and stars. Where is
the creature that winds and winds like this?
"Here we are." She has its shell in her palm,
I stand a touch away, this ocean
behind us. We stare at the snail shell.
Who has moved in? I open my hand wide:
a hermit crab steps off hers, jumps onto mine.

5.

"Nothing goes to waste," she sighs, "does it?"
We bend to the ground, warm sand on my knees,
I'm careful not to rub out the snail's leaves,
let the tide do that. The little hermit
is still in the cup of my sweaty hand,
not asleep but quieter. My young friend
and I smile, wouldn't her daughter like it.
Wouldn't mine? Hello, coming home this weekend?
"How old is your daughter?" Wouldn't she love
to know me, crawl into my lap? I would tell
her my stories of another day of
following a snail and finding its shell.
Then I could be full: my young woman and I,
laughing and walking with her child and mine.

# To My Son Who Is Getting Married In Two Days

"Hello, I'm home," you sing out each time
you return. How different when you leave,
sneaking out at night, leaving pieces
and little bits of you, an encrusted knife
on Shakespeare's shelf in my library,
last Monday's Sports on top of it; three
started rolls of toilet paper, two peach,
one white, and five hairy razors on my
sink; two coffee mugs on the piano;
the condoms; a few of your records; a few
poetry books; the black bag you blew
up when you needed to lengthen your obligato.
How considerate of you. This did mean
you'd be back again, yes, after I cleaned.

How considerate you were to try to make
each parting easy. Strange, isn't it, how
quick the rage, how fast the love, how soon
your call to let me know you are there, safe,
another journey away is over.
This morning after you left, I rolled up
the etching of the Brooklyn Bridge I found
for you last year; rescued your new T-square
from discarded papers; lifted and dusted
your trumpet case, your trumpet. Can it be
this is the last time you would have to do it,
the last time I would have to undo it.
Finished. My sweet, you don't live here anymore.
Soon you'll visit. For now, let's shut the door.

# Libation

Don't spill the wine: its blood red shadows
will evaporate quickly across cracks
of the courtyard near Herod's wall.
We know, we did it twice that day. Amen!
As our ten men chant the prayers
we wait aside with three wines, wait,

in the hot sun and the three wines wait
with us, still cool in our restless shadows.
Ah! Finally the Bar Mitzvah sings his prayers.
We smile as his voice cracks
and I did it? No, I didn't. Amen!
One bottle is cracked, wine running down wall,

two still intact to bless our boy at the wall.
He touches the sacred scrolls. We wait
for the serious grandfather's Amen!
Mazel tov! we shout. They parade their shadows
to us, not knowing one wine is dry in the cracks,
only two left to wet with, to hold our prayers.

Our young uncle grabs a bottle, sets it with a prayer
on the jagged rock of a low retaining wall.
Now! Two sacred wines run sweet into cracks.
What to do but joke, to bless the yard, to wait
for the rising bouquet. Out of the shadows
marches Aunt Fanny. Let us say Amen!

she shouts, to the Bar Mitzvah. Amen!
We toast, each with a drop of wine, with prayers
asking for long life. Why then the shadows
that soon reached the young uncle at his wall?
Did we make too much noise? We prayed as we waited.
But he spilled a life out into the cracks.

Aunt Fanny, who saved the one wine from the cracks,
is soon second, one stroke, she is down. Amen.
In the family album the uncle, Aunt Fanny, our boy, we wait
for the click with songs and laughter, with prayers
while we drink wine at the wall,

wine, spilling and seeping into shadow.

Now to stop a third from cracking. How? with this prayer?
Work on my Amen? Clean our drops at the wall?
Go, don't wait for me, it's cooler in the shadows.

# Euthanasia

The times she could have killed herself,
away from me down County Line Road,
my chasing after, and then her falling
through the ice in the pool, having to break
through it. And what about the blue jay's
tail feather sticking out of her mouth, and
she's running around the yard and I chase
her and out pops this stunned bird, the basset's
drool covering, almost drowning it.
When I think that she chewed my favorite
blue shoe and my cousin's good sunglasses
all in one day and there she stood wagging
that white-tipped tail of hers and now
she cannot stand, lies there, piles of her puke
all around her. I'm watching her die,
my old mother, too. Her flesh disappearing
around her rib cage and hers around hers,
every rib protruding, no hanging belly
anymore, her face sucked in, her nose
a pointer. I plead with her, don't make me
do it. Die. She is lying there in her
fetal position, her tongue out and dry,
first her chest wrenching and then all of her
wrenching and then she has to go and open
her eyes and I rub the top of her head
and then she has to go and rub back.

# IV. NOT AN ELEGY

## 84

### *Two Founds of Flesh*

It is not losing this thing that is frightening.
Plenty women I know have only one.
No, not the knife, not the blood, not the hole.
Think how much weight I will lose. This big thing.
You can't feel the lump with my brassiere on,
but when I take it off and the breast falls down,
you can feel it. Here, feel it, a long lump,
more than an inch, near the left nipple.
What? just the lump? No. What if they left
some thing, some little bit of the cancer.
Mind you, next March we would have celebrated
sixty years, your father and I and this breast.
No, my daughter, cut it off, I say,
take it, lop it off, take it, today.


### *The Anniversary*

Look where you drive—it's the anniversary
balloon that came with the flowers your sister
sent to us. See—look where you drive—Happy
60th Anniversary, Mom and Dad—still clear.
The gold isn't even peeling. I had it
folded in my pocketbook all the way
from Florida. The flowers were something—
a big arrangement—lasted for ten days,
and even when they died, the balloon
was still in the air smiling at us. Slowly
it started to come down and shrivel up.
One day it just dropped—that was that.
I tried to blow it up, so did Daddy.
Will you? for our anniversary party?

## *The Album*

You know who sent us a card? Maria,
Frank's daughter. We got it on Wednesday—
no, Sam, Wednesday. Tuesday we got the card
from Ariel, Lenny's grandson—it's
a paper card, he made it himself with his
computer—a genius that child. No, Sam,
couldn't be Wednesday, Wednesday was when
we got Maria's card. What are you talking
about. Tuesday, I played. Wednesday, I went—
don't tell me, Sam—to the beauty parlor,
So what was I saying. I got one thing
I want you to take back, a dust collector—
what do you call it? I can't remember a thing—
an album. I'll get earrings or a silver pin.

## *Mothers*

You know who we went to see yesterday?
Fay. Daddy and I finally got a ride.
What an actress—she pretends she's okay
but how, eating bits one at a time,
so bloated, her stomach hasn't worked yet.
Does she know it was malignant? She told
us it was a big tumor that they got all
out. When are they going to start the chemo?
When I walked into her room she couldn't
see who I was. I heard her whisper
"My Lois is here, my Lois." I said
"No, Fay, it's Lois' mother." I told her
I am not sharing you with her.
I said, "She's my daughter, not yours."

## *The Graduation*

Where were you last night? I'm fine now. You knew?
You didn't hear? I was sick all week. I caught
Daddy's cold and I fainted on Wednesday. No, now
I'm fine except I'm still coughing.
On Wednesday I thought for sure I couldn't go.
As long as I can still stand. I spoke
to your sister on Wednesday and Thursday.
She didn't call you? She knew I fainted.
Eighty-four and I'm still here and your father is here.
You spoke to the children this week? Sandy
must be excited. She didn't know I fainted?
I'm sure I should go. What time you coming
to pick us up? Eleven-thirty? So late?
How many times will I see Sandy graduate?

## *Brothers and Sisters*

Must have cost you a fortune, three in school,
must have been some job when they were babies,
so close in age. I couldn't have coped—
not the money or taking care of three
under three. How much did it cost—thousands?
Fifty? No, how could it. I can't believe
you could feed, bathe, get three ready for bed,
I couldn't. You're fertile just like me.
You're still getting it? you be careful—
there were two other times I conceived—
twice in the eight years between you and Claire,
two strong boys to watch over my two girls.
In the thirties they called it a D and C,
today they say abortion, don't you see?

## The Birthday

Where were you last night? Again? A meeting
at the school? Stop working so hard, *tochter,*
Oh— I meant to tell you—you know those beads,
the gorgeous ones I bought in Florida?
Did I tell you—my Thursday game never
says a word about them—all the time I wore them.
But my black beads—oh, onyx? the ones
you just gave me Tuesday for my eighty-fourth
birthday—oy, I'm getting there--those they loved.
Do you believe it? I wore them with my new gray
blouse—it really looks good on me. Eight
dollars in Florida—I couldn't have
found such a blouse for eighty in Lakewood.
Come over tonight. I'm almost out of milk.


## The Funeral

What kind of funeral is that, at the grave,
no funeral parlor, no eulogy,
only a prayer at the grave, poor Fay,
she never expected to go so quickly.
I don't want to be buried like a dog.
I want a big funeral, a big chapel.
Invite all my ORT friends from Crestwood.
I want you to call the whole family,
your aunts and uncle in Florida, too.
Should we have it in New York or here;
who do I know in New York. Let's do
it here in New Jersey. Show me you care.
Where's aisle nine? Papa wrote it down for
prune juice. You got four apples? No, get more.

# Eight, at Least

1.

Thirty years of thinking he's dying, this time
he's really dying—my father, my old
father—each time he grays to the top, his bald
head gray, his eyes roll up, then drops into my
arms. All this time was he saying: look at me,
daughter, for a change, for once, look at me.
I am taller than you think. I'm smarter, too.
Watch me look dead. Watch, I'll collect my dues.
Let me count the times he's done it. At our
cousin's engagement party. At Mark's
Bar Mitzvah. In shul on Yom Kippur, four years
in a row. Seven, if I count Florida,
but I wasn't there. Eight, at least, if I say
he planned this one on my son's wedding day.

2.

He did it so well on his grandson's
day, waited to watch me lead this boy
by his sweaty hand for the walk out,
watched the bride leading her family gown,
my old father sat squinting at us
under the blue and white tent until I
could get off the line and lift bubbles
of cool champagne to my lips and I
could feel how cool inside me, and are they
man and wife, these sweet things, and I shall miss
them, and then my old father started to gray
to the top, then white, as he rolled his eyes
at me. "I don't feel well," he muttered,
a crowd around him, he scared, lying there.

3.

Again, he lay there, a crowd around.
Again, I didn't dance with the groom, instead climbed
into the ambulance to wipe the crumbs
from his face, stroke his head, hold his hands;
sit at his side in the hospital laughing
him back, watching the monitor recording

his beats, his rhythms charging the machines,
his hand still, our eyes staring at the screens.
Oh Father, what do I do about you?
Do I dare to let you go to shul? You must?
And that party next month on Long Island,
you want to be there, too? Pass out there, too?
No, you didn't die this Sunday. "Not my time
yet," you sing out. Father, I think it's mine.

# Their Quality of Life

1.

My father stares ahead, chewing his gum
with a square jaw; he knows this is his last
chance to read again, damn the diabetes.
Suppose the doctor says, no, you are not
a candidate for low vision care, too bad.
And if you are, how much will it cost, "Thousands,"
I said. "No, how can that be?" His gum must
be rubber by now, those clicking dentures
faster and faster on it. "What kind of glasses
costs thousands of dollars?" The doctor's turn
now, shows him a pair, draws pictures three times,
takes him to a mirror and still he asks,
"How much?" Finally he has the answer
he doesn't want: One thousand, two hundred.

2.

That my father's glasses were on order,
had everything to do with my asking
my mother if she wanted me to help her
investigate a hearing aid. Her first
question was her usual one, "What? What are
you saying?" Then her request, "Talk louder,
I can't hear you when you talk so low."
She worried about the details:
who to see, where to go, the cost, how to
wear her hair so the thing wouldn't show.
Finally we went, first for the hearing test,
then to the office where they took the mold
of her right ear, showed her how to put it in,
take it out, turn it softer, louder, louder.

3.

Sign here on this line. "No, I don't think so."
He isn't convinced the glasses would work.
He had to talk to his wife, he had to think
about it, he had to think about the money,
which C.D. to cash in, he hated to do
that, but what could he do, what else to do?
Yes, he ordered them, but does he own them?
He didn't know they would look funny like that,
that he would have to hold the paper so close,
how can he write checks with that thing on his nose.
"They made him so dizzy, I was afraid
he was going to faint," my mother said
the night she told me, "You know that eye doctor,
what's his name, gave us eight hundred dollars back."


4.

"I can't turn that little little button.
This way? No? That?" over and over until
this patient man, a saint, says to her, "I'll fix
the volume for you in one place." "Oy, it's
so ugly, in my ear?" She will never
put it in, will she, it is going to sit
in her bureau, her unused handkerchiefs.
Her next demand, "I want a week's trial
before I pay anything." So, she's not
going to get one after all, so I am
Telemachus, the child who knows not how
to help. If she's decided, let it be.
Don't shout, why hurt my voice. Smile.Tell her,
Why then, Mother, cancel the order.

# Nails

When the phone rang and it was my father and she was out
of surgery, had gotten through the anaesthesia, had
done well, they had affixed into her cleaned out hip joint a
prosthetic ball, a new head and neck, had taken out all
the bones shattered by the spread of her cancer, a new
head and neck for her shattered femur, a new hip, titan-
ium hammered into her bone, finally I could run
out into the rain, over, down Third Avenue into
Friday's heaviest rain. It's over, I wanted to shout, she's
out of surgery, my eighty-six year old mommy made
it. What does it mean to anyone else in Friday's rain,
to the Chinese girl in the Nail Shop who smiles when I say
it, her round face down almost to the table where I rest
my hands. She must be in the recovery room, the tube
down her throat, is she gasping? Old red leaks out onto my
fingers. She sponges it up, touches my broken nail, glues
it down, blows on it, her breath spicy and warm on me. Want
linen, it's stronger she says, yes, her new hip must be
raging. Another coat of glue, the linen pulled and cut, pushed
down, glued down, another, and more warm garlic and pepper,
a spicy anaesthesia, I try to wet my scratchy tongue,
my nine fingers soaking in blue and white bubbles, one
out, getting stronger and stronger and thicker. She must have
eaten lunch, they wouldn't let her eat mushrooms and
broccoli sauteed in hot oil, sticky steamed rice,
hot red peppers sizzling in the oil, into the linen,
and garlic in glue, into glucose, into us, us too.

# Tivoli

It isn't at all apparent when we arrive at Tivoli,
the new sleek dining spot on Sunny Isles Boulevard
in North Miami that Saturday night at six o'clock,
but when a woman in beige bouffant hair turns, as I order
a B&G Partager, and I see that a black patch covers
her left eye, I know the wines are overpriced, the menu small,
only four entrees. My mother feels daring tonight, lets
our young waiter wet the bottom of her glass on her first
night out since radiation therapy. I know my mother needs
the walker—I see the woman two tables down in her
wheel chair, her right arm limp in her lap, watching
my father conscientiously dipping crudites in an interesting
garlic mustard—but I am trying to convince my mother,
get out, who is perfect? My mother picks at a romaine leaf
vinaigrette garnished with croutons, while I beg her to be
satisfied with feeling good, and I know them when I look up,
the Feins, Mrs., hair teased and sprayed, Mr. leaning on her,
shuffling slowly, how are you? and how are you? What food!
What service, just terrific! I had duck l'orange, you ordered?
You can't have sugar? Try the veal francaise, just a little salt
they told me, but I was afraid. You enjoy! Slowly the Feins
walk their way out, his right arm linked into her left, his
right leg stiff, her left tight behind. How handsome, how sweet
and milky that primavera. Is it for the wheel chair woman?
Who ordered steak grilled on mesquite, how daring, not spicy,
I assure the four canes who just walked in and sat down
at the next table. What polished handles, what pleats in
the crisp white cotton slacks, all four tanned into the inner-
most ridges of their cheeks. One leans over, would I read
the menu to them, it's so dark in here, just the entrees,
only four or five and I know them by heart, I know what is
best for the four of them, for us, too. As I recite what
I know, my entree, at last, here it is, steaming. Carefully
I push the pastry to one side, slide the slippery flesh
onto my fork, into my mouth. What a wonderful lemon sole.

# Passover

She *can't* pee in her pants,
she's hooked up to a plastic bag,
I tell the airlines. *What* permission to fly,
is this a class trip, I ask them.
I promised her, I tell them, her own home
for the holiday, home by Wednesday night.
Do they care? Delta Airlines?
She's never missed a seder, I tell them,
she's eighty-six.
                I'm flying, aren't I?
                Whose room is this?
                Is this an airplane?
                I cleaned myself out
                today, what a difference.
                Will I have a chair
                like this one at home?
Yesterday the surgeon said today or tomorrow,
check out her heart, her hip.
Where is he? At noon I check at the desk.
They don't know where or what.
                What is this, a gown?
                Is this what I wear
                when I go on the plane?
                Will you dress me?
                What will I wear,
                tell me again.
                How fast I forget
                the whole story.
An hour later they tell me
it's the social worker who will see us
today or tomorrow. That means not tomorrow,
we don't go home tomorrow. Another night
and another day here and another night,
the first seder gone and the second.
                Eat? I'll eat.
                What's that noise?
                Tell me what to do
                and I'll do it.
                Is it lunch?
                No lunch.
                No, no, no, no no.
So when Sue Anne Tanner, MSW, walks in at four
and says, sure I'll get you the letter,

I'll arrange the Medi-van and the records
for tomorrow, I'm surprised, and when
the line isn't busy and the seats are
available and I reserve them, I'm surprised.
                While I'm sitting here
                I should brush my teeth.
                Here, take them,
                wash them.
                Where are they?
                Give them back to me.
                Let me do it,
                    you're not doing it right.
I need to get her things ready,
they'll tell me visiting hours are over,
when hello, here comes her cardiologist
who says no, not tomorrow, no to the next day.
Am I surprised? No, I'm numb,
and I'm still numb when my mother asks,
                Are we there?
                Are we there yet?

# I'm Dying,
## You're Not

Doctor help me I'm dying I'm dying
   You're not dying
Iam Iam Iam I'm going fast
   You're not ...
I'm dying come over now you're a doctor I can't breathe
   ...listening to me
Why won't you come you're my son-in-law
   You're not dying
No? let me talk to my daughter

Come backcome backcome back NOW
   I just walked in the door
Come back I'm dying Come back NOW
   I just saw you a few minutes ago
I don't have long to live
   I haven't eaten yet It's late I'm tired
Come back or you'll be sorry COME BACK
   Here's your granddaughter

COMEBACKCOMEBACKCOMEBACK
   What's the matter Nana
I'mdyingI'mdyingI'mdying
   Nana we are going to eat now
NONO YOU DON'T EAT NOW
   You're not listening
I'll never forgive you if you don't come back now
   Listen to me sleep now go to sleep
Comeover
   NoNana
Comeover
   Tomorrow
Nonow
   Nanano

Come
   later
over
   Mother
Come
   No
over
   No
now

# What's Left of the Moon and My Mother

Earlier this morning, the moon, a sliver of
a white tip, kept pushing a few flimsy clouds away.
A waning moon, isn't it, my mother a waning moon,
all in one day a little better, a bit worse.
Today for example, when I suggest the Palms—
we've eaten there this year, twice before she got sick,
once since she's feeling better and getting around—
she knows it has been raining hard all day, but she wants
to go, waits for me in her raincoat, announces she won't
wear her boots and she won't take her cane. She will hold
onto me as we walk down the path. She promises she won't
fall. It's not until I drive five miles that she asks
in a rush, did I take the cane, and where are her boots,
what did I mean she decided no, she wouldn't wear them,
it's raining so hard, and where are we going? Six miles away
we talk about the broiled scrod she likes so much at this
place. Are you hungry, I ask her. She answers, you know
I can't regulate my stomach, for months now. I can't.
Here we go again, her bowel movements, again. I didn't
ask you that, Mother. Yes, I did, that's why she isn't
hungry, but she eats anyway. She taps my arm, broiled what?
Broiled what do I like? Scrod. Broiled scrod, that's what
she should order, I tell her. Not swordfish? No, too dry,
it was too dry last time. Ten miles and we turn into
the long driveway, pull into the handicapped spot, walk
slowly in the rain into the restaurant. I hang up our wet
coats, we're seated. The bread warm and moist, she loves it
that way, the waitress brings me a glass of wine, I'm starting
to relax, her cheeks are pink and warm, she was hungry
that's all. No, that's not all. The waitress takes her order
and as she tells her what she wants I remember her screams
in the hospital and rehab center, her screaming even after
she came home and I would have to run and calm her,
her screaming all night, her not knowing, her head
a whirlwind and so noisy, she said. I remember
the night I brought the tiny white pills she would use
until she was used to the nights, I didn't dare tell her
I'd have to ask the vet for more pills--they were not
prescribed for her, they were the dying cat's, my little
little little pills she named them, his not hers.
She won't let me forget. She orders swordfish.

# Not an Elegy, Yet

Once the wind lifted my hand
and my hand met hers.
We thought how lovely to be
content, to pull silent steps
side by side.

Today when her pink scalp
lay exposed, her hairs wet
and thin—gray ropes,
I gently massaged shampoo
into her shiny skin.
And my fingers ran through
her thin hairs.
Mother sighed and sighed.

Later we thought how lovely to be
here to sip tea,
sip after sip,
our choice.

## *Dies supremus*

She's dead
Is she
in the ground
I can't tell
I can't see her
Why is it
I miss her
so much

Yes
my child
No
No
I know
I don't know
too much
too

too much
I'll miss you
why is it
I know
You're not cold
cold
she is
I don't know

Don't run
Am I
I am
you can't run
fast enough
how much
you miss me
how much

No
I'm her little one
now
yes

No

how much
you miss me
how much
fast enough
I can't run
I'm dead
Am I
Don't run

I don't cry
She is
cold
you're not cold
I know
so much
I'll miss you
too much

no
you know


Yes
Now
I'm her little one


so much
I miss her
so much
I can't see her
I can't tell
in the ground
Is she
She is

# V. QUESTIONS

# The Question

Some breezes are stirring in us, some heat
in our fingers lightly braided. We talk
as we walk into a tree lined street
in Jerusalem, an ordinary walk.
But when an armored car climbs the curb,
stops, opens wide, its bomb squad stops us,
searches us, our path, all around us, THERE
IN THE PAINT CANS, there behind us, we must
be still. Slowly, they lift the cans and go.
Still dazed, we back up to our last moment,
up close, two rusty circles on the pavement.
I run my finger along the stains,
what were we saying? what was the question
you were asking? why didn't I listen?

# Is This the Poem?

Is it in the tram half away now,
is it, coming down from the Rockpile
on the side of the mountain, cutouts,
stretches of green, paths for the skiers,
is it in mariposa lilies,
their dark blue markings,
Indian paintbrushes so close
to the ground that I could not miss them
as I watched my step, heel first, always
dig in with the heel into the steep
gravel and rock path up the mountain,
what is this, feeling faint, lying there,
saying, but this is not the poem,
knowing I'd find it on the way back,
saying it is this three year old
on the tram who watches me eat plums,
her tongue wetting her lips, this copper-
colored child, this little wild flower,
and I'm admiring her and her yellow
plastic barrettes and her five bangles,
the center one turquoise to match
her overalls, the two outer
as purple as the label on her front,
and she's showing me how dirty
she got her sneaks on Squaw Mountain,
I'm showing her mine and then her eyes
on my plum, may I, I ask her father,
how white his skin and he's saying,
sure, and I pull one out of the plastic
bag, no, this is not yet the poem,
is it, Matt, a little taller,
a little darker comes over and
watches the two of us and I ask
his father is this it, is this the last,
how many children do you have,
he laughs at me, at least twelve, and
I say too bad for the other ten,
and I laugh, at least I have one
for Matt, my last plum, and here comes
his mother and she smiles at me
and asks him, did you say thank you,
and the five of us ride the car down
into the valley, the clouds, pine trees,

even trees one at a time on ledges,
tasting plum again and snow melting
in shallow paths, and lilies and
paintbrushes, and there, it is, at last.

# Who Knows?

## *the daughter?*

My brother doesn't understand shit,
knows how to play bridge, runs to tournaments.
You tell him how I'm living, you're his wife.
I dread coming home at night, as I drive
onto my street I want to cry. It sucks.
The other night was the worst. I was sick,
exhausted. Pop kept after me, shouting,
"Give me back my money, I know you
stole it!" screaming and screaming at me even
after I shut my bedroom door, half the night,
until Mom finally coaxed him to bed.
Let him go live with my brother and you,
don't you think? I tried. I did everything
I could to make him happy, everything.

## *the daughter-in-law?*

Pop, my husband has always been the good son,
still wants to hold you. When he visits you
he holds your wrinkled hands, smoothes back the hair
from your face. He listens when you shout,
"Who stole the money, you?" when Mother
weeps, "Get me out, my life is a dark hole."
He tries to find the right words to comfort
you. "You can't live alone. Our apartment
is too small. I'll be only a taxi-ride
away from you, minutes away." He fights
with you to eat dinner, brushes the crumbs
from your mouth, dips his elbow in before he
washes you, powders you to make you sweet,
covers you with pale sunlight, with your sheets.

## *the father?*

How can I be? Sometimes I don't know
at all. Sometimes I know I'm not good. The old
problem is better, but I'm still wearing
the diapers. I'm always afraid I'll start
to ooze again. Tell me, son, can it be worse?
No, not the oozing. The knowing or not.
I'm beginning to think not knowing is
better. I don't want to know my own
are stealing my money. Her father stole some
too, when we were in Florida. She screams
at me and she says I'm the one screaming.
When I don't know, everyone is calm, at peace
and I go for a walk with your mother, Rose.
Then, they tell me, now you're fine, but who knows.

## *the son?*

My sister thinks she can think for me,
thinks she can make all the decisions.
She decides my life. She tells me what to do.
I'm the good brother, the good son, so
I do it. Not this time. She's not dropping
you off in our apartment for a month.
She's doing it for the money. Did you know,
Mom, you were paying her to stay in her house?
She's the one who brought you up
from Florida. If she brings you to us
I'm putting you in a hotel. She's going
to call tonight, that's what I'm telling her.
When is my birthday? On Saturday.
How many candles on the cake? Fifty-eight.

## *the mother?*

No matter what he calls it, hotel, motel,
it's a nursing home. I want to go back
to Florida. If he can't go back, put
him in it, not me. I want to go back,
I don't want to stay in her house anymore,
I want to be in my own place again.
I want to do my own cooking, I won't burn
the place down. I want to do my own cleaning,
I won't move the furniture. I want
to do my own shopping, I'll be careful
on the steps. One pinned hip is enough.
Isn't sixty-two years enough with one man?
Let him scream at his daughter, not at me.
I'll tell him, no more do this, do that, for me.

## *her friend?*

Be smart, butt out. I tell you, don't mix
in whenever your son and daughter fight. Don't
interfere. If it hurts, walk out on them,
close both front doors, rock on the porch, rock
out here, up and back, look up and then close
your ears, whistle a song, stare ahead, fake
a laugh when they scream, start praying they
won't have permanent scars. Wave to me.
Ask, how are you today? Button and
unbutton your sweater, like this. After all,
first comes the fighting, then the trusting,
then the listening and soon, God willing,
they'll hear you, listen to you say what you need.
Your own place? Sure. Then they'll let you leave.

# Way To Go

The night before Cousin Abe dies, he will not
sleep in the guest room in his daughter's new house.
He starts his customary roaming. His shouting.
The children tell him, Grandpa, we'll help you.
They set him on the floor in the living room,
cover him, sing to him, sing to him all night
the lullabies he sang to them, maybe
four years ago. Still, he will not sleep,
but he is calmer and quieter. Towards dawn
Abe shaves, trims his toe nails, puts on new underwear,
new socks, his best pinstriped shirt, tie, jacket, pants,
and lays himself out on that bed prepared
for him in his daughter's house. Children, go. Please.
Go and play, he begs them. I'm ready. I'll sleep.

# Multiples

It's the blue spruce she likes to look at
from her window. Twenty-five years old
and twenty-five feet high now. Twenty-five
and twenty-five are fifty, but she is
more than fifty now. Sometimes she likes to sit
at her bedroom window. She should count its arms.

Today she likes to sit in the yard.
How many people have a Sir Harry Lauder
walking stick. Someone will have to cut
those sticks out. She had better cut
the straight stalks today. One of the wiggly
branches broke off. If she finds three more
like this one on the ground, she'll buy
that black glass vase. She writes a note:
1. cut out all straight sticks 2. find more
squiggles (at least three) 3. buy vase.
She adds: 4. How old is Spruce?

Should she buy the black glass vase.
One year she grew silver dollars—
what a delicacy. On Third Avenue the man
wanted twenty dollars for one branch.
She'll search the house, what could she
have done with them. Hello, here they'll be—
dusty and torn, but here they are.
She would not have discarded them.
Who would sleep in this room now.
Where's her list: 2. find more squiggles
(at least three) 4. consider silver dollars.

Where would she keep the vase, anyway.
She makes room on the piano, pushes
an old photo away. She stops to look
how wavy her mother's hair was, and
how dark and how thick—growing out
like that. Her daughter's like that, too.
How she might love to run fingers
into the tight curls. Last week
they trimmed the hairs that fell down
a little faster, the straighter ones.
5. New combs, of course. She adds them.